# From The Mist The Angels Came

Inspired Writings
By
Sandra J Yearman

## SERAPHIM PUBLISHING LLC

## WE WILL BRING LIGHT TO ALL THE DARK PLACES

Registered trademark-
Sandra J Yearman
Seraphim Publishing
438 Water St. Cambridge, WI 53523

Copyright © 2008 Sandra J Yearman
Produced in the United States of America
Author : Sandra J Yearman
Editor: Sandra J Yearman
Cover Design by Sandra J Yearman
Layout and design by Sandra J Yearman

All rights reserved. No part of this book may be reproduced, stored in or introduced into a retrieval system, or transmitted, in any form or by any means, electronic or mechanical, including photocopying or recording or otherwise copied for public or private use—other than for "fair use" as brief quotations embodied in articles and reviews—without written permission from the author.

Library of Congress Control Number: 2009907516
ISBN: 978-0-9841506-2-5
First Edition

From The Mist Came Angels
The Army That God Sent
To Rescue All The Victims
His Promises, As Meant
Amen
Amen
Amen

# CONTENTS

## DEDICATION

From The Mist The Angels Came..................7
The Word........................................................9
Joy.................................................................12
His Will.........................................................14
We Are Your Holy Children........................16
We Love........................................................18
I Need More..................................................20
House Of The Lord.......................................21
With My Voice.............................................22

## SEEKING LIGHT IN THE DARKNESS

Reborn..........................................................25
God's Home..................................................29
Behind Time.................................................32
Tear...............................................................35
Lord Whisper Into My Heart ......................38
Armies Of The Night....................................40
That's The Way Of The World....................43
I Am Lost......................................................45
Old And Broken Men ..................................47

# CONTENTS

For All Creation's Sake ................................ 50
What If God Looked The Other Way ............ 52
Loss .............................................................. 55
Love .............................................................. 57
I Am A Stranger Even To Me ....................... 61
Help Us To Pray ........................................... 63
God, Are You Still Here ................................ 65
A Sanctuary Of Angels ................................. 67
Broken Wings ............................................... 70
Voices Raised In Prayer ................................ 72
God Can You Use Me .................................. 76

## COMING HOME

Coming Home .............................................. 79
Created By God's Hand ................................ 80
A Celebration Of Angels .............................. 82
Return To Thee ............................................ 85
Amidst The Cries And Chaos ....................... 87

# Dedication

# From The Mist The Angels Came

From the mist
The Angels came
To save creation
In Heaven's name

The King of Angels
The ancient Lord
Came with blessings
The dove and the sword

And all creation
Bows before
The King of Kings
The Angels soar

The Lamb, the Lion
The Dove and the Sword
Forgives His children
And creation soars

The King of Kings
The Angels sing

Amen Amen Amen

# The Word

Angels sang their praises
As the Word touched us with
His Grace
Timeless is the Spirit
Eternal is the faith

The Word walked among us
The Word became flesh
The Word suffered our
punishment
Through Salvation we are Blessed

His actions were God's Living Words
His Holy truths revealed
The Love and Grace of Heaven
God's covenants were sealed

Angels sang their praises
As the Word touched us with
His Grace
Timeless is the Spirit
Eternal is the faith

The Word that filled these dark
nations
The Light that showed us our way
Home
The Protector, Shepherd of the sheep
The Lamb whose blood did Atone

On the throne He judges nations
On His wings we will soar
The righteous will fear no evil
Raised from darkness, chains no more

Angels sang their praises
As the Word touched us with
His Grace
Timeless is the Spirit
Eternal is the faith

On the right Hand of the Father
For us He did conquer death
Freed His children from their captors
Gave us life, for this we are Blessed

He is with us always
His Spirit never leaves
He is the Love of Heaven
He Blessed those who believe

Amen Amen Amen

# Joy

I am young and free
The sun shines warmly on me

I kiss the wind and with it fly
I love this day, my Lord, His Will

My joys are overflowing
My heart is full of Song

I am filled with the Holy Spirit
I am dancing in the air

My happiness is breathtaking
I am overwhelmed
With my love, with my life, with my Lord

Thank You Lord for all my blessings
Thank You Lord, thank You

Amen Amen Amen

# His Will

Let His Will
Be sung by all our voices
Let His Will
Guide our earthly choices

Let His Presence
Saturate our souls
Let His Presence
Make us whole

Let His Being
Fill our hearts
Let His Being
Be where we start

Let His Love
Heal us all
And beckon us
With Heaven's call

Amen Amen Amen

# We Are Your Holy Children

God our Holy Father in Heaven
Forgive us for the darkness we seek
Forgive us and carry us this day

We surrender to Your Love
To Your Will
To Your Holiness

You are our Lord
Our Redeemer
Our Salvation

We are Your Holy children
We are part of Your Holy creation

We thank You for all of our many
Blessings
We thank You for the Miracles You
bring to our lives
We thank You for Your Loving
Forgiveness
We sing Your praises
Alleluia, Alleluia, Alleluia

Amen Amen Amen

# We Love

We seek You our Lord
We call You our Father
We pray to You Holy One
We seek You

We worship You our God
We adore You our Savior
We praise You our All
We worship

We fall to our knees
We open our hearts
We raise our voices
We love

We seek
We worship
We love
You are our All

Amen Amen Amen

# I Need More

God I need more of Your Light in my life
I need more of Your Song
I need to feel Your Presence with me daily
I need Your warmth

God I need more of Your Love in my life
I need more of Your Holiness
I need more of Your Peace, Your Power, Your Grace

Holy One I need more...
I need a life filled with You

Amen Amen Amen

# House Of The Lord

As we ask to dwell in the House of the Lord
So too, should we ask the Lord to dwell
In our homes
In our hearts
In our places of business
In our lives

May our doors never close to the Lord our God
May our homes and hearts be filled with His Light
May our lives always be dedicated to His Will

Lord consume us with You

Amen Amen Amen

# With My Voice

At Your feet I honor You my Lord
At Your feet I sing Your praise
At Your feet I cry tears of redemption
At Your feet

On my knees I will worship
My God
My Savior
My Redeemer
On my knees

With my voice
I will stand before You
I will sing Your Song
I will pray
With my voice

With my heart
I will surrender
I will surrender
I will surrender

With my heart

My Father

Amen Amen Amen

# Seeking Light In The Darkness

# Reborn

Crippled by his burdens
Heavy with the weight
The shell of a man
Was filled with doubt and hate

He had a chance encounter
With a child ever so small
An encounter that would change his life
And remind him of it all

Disfigured by his demons
He told of a time long ago
When he became a man of God
A path he no longer knows

As he told his story
He repeatedly apologized
For choosing a path of Holiness
He now saw with different eyes

The child listened
To what he said
And realized the man
Was walking among the dead

She took his hand
And smiled
And said 'now'
'Let us walk awhile'

'Do not apologize'
'For God is needed in this place'
'So much darkness'
'Terror and hate'

'If you can bring'
'But a little light'
'To dissolve'
'The darkness of this night'

'Then God will bless you'
'As you know'
'For through His Son'
'He told us so'

As the child
Took his hand
She reminded him
Why he became a Holy man

Amen Amen Amen

# God's Home

We care about our families
We care about our homes
We care about our children
We care about our own

We take care of
We provide for
We protect
We pray for
Our families, our lives

What if we thought about the
World as our Home
And all God's creations as our family

Would it change the way we see
Would it change the way we think
Would it change the way we hate

What if we thought about the
World as our home
And all God's creations as our family

Would there be genocide
Would there be hunger
Would there be destruction

What if we looked at the world
As if it was God's Home
And all His creations our family

What would we save
What would we rescue
What would we stand before

What if we looked at the world
As if it was God's Home
And all His creations our family

Would we love differently
Would we pray differently
Would we forgive differently

What if we looked at the world
As if it was God's home...

Amen Amen Amen

# Behind Time

Filled with stress and anguish
Always behind time
Too busy to enjoy life
Too busy for the sublime

God in all the frenzy
Let it be Your Voice that I hear
When I am lost in the chaos
I need to have You near

Racing ever farther
Yet always moving in place
Priorities askew
Everything done in haste

God in all the frenzy
Let it be Your Voice that I hear
When I am lost in the chaos
I need to have You near

Too busy to take value
Too busy to take stock
Grown and lost before it is realized
Filled with anger and shock

God in all the frenzy
Let it be Your Voice that I hear
When I am lost in the chaos
I need to have You near

Families lose their meanings
When no members are in the home
No time for love or laughter
Isolated they roam

God in all the frenzy
Let it be Your Voice that I hear
When I am lost in the chaos
I need to have You near

Amen Amen Amen

# Tear

Why must the children cry
There is no laughter
They die
The world goes on

Another war
The tears come no more
There are none left
The children die

The victims of greed
The victims of politics
The victims of bigotry
The victims of man

The children of all creation cry this night
Lord help us to see through the fear
Lord help us to see what is real

We take Your gifts and distort, abuse and destroy them
We remake them in the image of man
Lord help us to see through the illusions

Lord forgive us our sins
Lord forgive us our guilt
Lord forgive us our fears

Lord please bring Your Holy Light into our dark worlds

Lord save Your children here

Amen Amen Amen

# Lord Whisper Into My Heart

Lord hold my hand
Lead me down the path that You
would have me walk

Lord hold my hand
Steady me when I am falling

Lord hold my hand
Comfort me when I am in agony

Lord whisper into my heart
Guide me in making Holy choices

Lord whisper into my heart
And let Your Will be done

Lord whisper into my heart
Use me as an instrument of Your Will

Lord carry me
When I can no longer walk

Lord carry me
When I can no longer speak

Lord carry me Home
When my time has come

Amen Amen Amen

# Armies Of The Night

The armies of the dead
Tried to take the night
They battered creation
Strike after strike

Their advance seemed imminent
Many of God's children were calling
them near
The fate of creation
The lives filled with fear

God sent His Angels
Led by the Son
To save all creation
A battle He won

But God's children
Still cried to the night
They took on the fear
The horror, the fright

God in His Mercy
Still loves them today
He blessed them and saved them
And showed them the Way

But much of creation
Is confused and lost
They forgot the reason
Jesus died on the cross

To show us
That we could conquer the night
To overcome death
Terror and fright

But God in His Justice
Lets us choose our way
The darkness of night
Or the Glory of day

Amen Amen Amen

# That's The Way Of The World

That's the way of the world
War
Murder
Hatred
The sirens never stop

That's the way of the world
Fear
Deception
Misuse of power
The cries never stop

That's the way of the world
Darkness
Defiling
Victims
The pain never stops

Heavenly Father help us to transcend the horror
The darkness, the boundaries of this world

Heavenly Father, help us to disempower the darkness

Heavenly Father
Fill us with the Holy Spirit
Engulf us with Your Holy Light
Show Your Mercy upon us

Amen Amen Amen

# I Am Lost

Lord I have been injured
I have been victimized
I can not feel life within me any more

I am numbed
I am traumatized
I am dead

I have felt nothing for so long
That even feeling pain would be a relief
I sit motionless as the darkness attacks me

I would cry in pain
But I no longer have a voice
I stopped fighting long ago

I am lost
I am terrorized
I am dead inside

God please heal me
Heavenly Father please save me

Amen Amen Amen

# Old And Broken Men

Old and broken men
Their faces marked and worn
By years and experiences
By lives unfulfilled
By dreams turned to nightmares

They have lost their hope
They have lost their souls
They have lost their conscious

Memories of their choices
Memories of their deeds
Memories of their journeys

Bring horror
Bring terror
Bring remorse

Their fears have hollowed them out
Their lifeless bodies go through the motions
They choose not to overcome the darkness in their beings

God help us to live the lives You blessed us with
Help us to reach our potential, our destinies

Help us to overcome the darkness within and without

God remind us we are Your children

Amen Amen Amen

## For All Creation's Sake

All of man's decisions
Affects the life we see
Every aspect of creation
Every gift sent from Thee

When will mankind learn
To think before it acts
To see the repercussions
To gather all the facts

A decision in a boardroom
Made with greed and haste
Can destroy innumerable lives
Can lay the world to waste

No man has all the answers
So why do they not see
The strength in all decisions
Should be influenced by Thee

Put it to the Heavens
The decisions you must make
Ask for God to guide you
For all creation's sake

Amen Amen Amen

# What If God Looked The Other Way

They tell me
I should hate you
I should destroy you
I should ignore you

Your pain
Your life
Your struggle

They tell me there is a hierarchy to
God's creations
They tell me
To look the other way
Not to be bothered
Our differences are meant to
separate us

What if God
Hated us
Destroyed us
Ignored us

What if God
Looked the other way
Couldn't be bothered
Saw us as different from what He created

God remind us of the Holiness You created in each of us

God remind us of the Holiness You created in all of Your creation

If Jesus took the time to care for others
If Jesus took the time to feed others
If Jesus took the time to love and teach others

Why can't we...

Amen Amen Amen

# Loss

So many things left unsaid
Timeless words, unforgotten thoughts
My mind still strays to things I wanted to say
Things I should have said

But, I was afraid, now I am lost
My fears kept me from saying
The words my heart sang

My fears kept me from happiness
My fears held me back

Now I am filled with regret
I am immobilized with pain
My guilt perpetuates my mourning

God teach us not to allow our fears to destroy our lives

God teach us not to allow our fears to influence our decisions

God teach us to share love whenever we can

Amen Amen Amen

# Love

His bones ached from
The cold and the damp
Of a place he created
A place in which he was trapped

The maze bewildered
Him for so long
He had forgotten his way
He had forgotten the Song

Accustomed to darkness
His eyes could no longer see
He chose to hide
He chose to flee

In the darkness
A light appeared
To let him know
That God was near

Disfigured and crippled
From the weight of his deeds
His guilt drove him to madness
His fears and his needs

There is no place so dark
There is no place you can flee
That the Father can not find you
Can not bring you back to Three

In the darkness
A light appeared
To let him know
That God was near

And in His wisdom
God healed this man
Gave him clear sight
Held him in His hands

In the darkness
A light appeared
To let him know
That God was near

This man was cleansed
By God's Love and Might
Reborn in the day
No longer a victim of the night

He blossomed and flourished
And found great strength
And became a leader
Of Light in this place

In the darkness
A light appeared
To let him know
That God was near

Amen Amen Amen

# I Am A Stranger Even To Me

God I am screaming Your Name
Are You listening
Will You hear me

I don't know who I am
I don't recognize myself
I am a stranger even to me

I am a victim of my own choices
I am a prisoner of my own deeds
My fears torture me
The darkness within me obliterates
Your Holy Light

Lord Jesus save me
Teach me to pray
Give me the words
Open my heart
Show me how to bring You into my life

Jesus save me
Before it is too late

Amen Amen Amen

# Help Us To Pray

God help us to pray for
Those without voices
Those who are lost
Those who are victimized
Those who are traumatized

God teach us to pray for those who are filled with darkness
That they may be healed and cleansed with Your Holy Light
God help us to pray for the dead and the dying

God help us to pray for all of Your creations
For each and every life form in this world
That You may shine Your Face upon us

Amen Amen Amen

# God Are You Still Here

God are You still here
I have not spoken to You in so long

It's not that I have forgotten about You
I never make time for You
I never include You
I never pray to You

God if You are willing to listen
Please show me the Way

I am so out of control
I have made so many mistakes
So many poor choices

Please God
Show me the answer
Show me the Way

Amen Amen Amen

# A Sanctuary Of Angels

Enveloped in the wings of an Angel
He was saved that day
When God heard his cries to Heaven
When God saved his life that way

The troops were surrounded in ambush
Dark eyes lurking in the night
When a warrior prayed to Heaven
When God saved them with His Might

And a sanctuary of Angels
Engulfed the men that night
And protected them in the darkness
And brought them God's Holy Light

The leader brave and honored
Surrendered to his Lord
The night the enemy out-numbered them
The night he saw Heaven's Sword

A miracle happened in the dark night
That no man could explain
Enveloped in the wings of Angels
Destruction of the insane

The leader brave and honored
Asked God to save his men
To stand with them against darkness
To bring insanity to an end

When the Morning Star had risen
And the darkness turned to day
The leader brave and honored
Saw that God had made a better Way

Amen Amen Amen

# Broken Wings

Broken wings
Broken Spirits
Broken men

We are so frail
We seek to mask our fears
With false images and aggression

We seek to cover our weakness
With self importance

We seek to cloak our darkness
With masked glory

We are not God, yet there are those
Among us who would claim
That glory
That power
That holiness

Jesus held up a mirror to our darkness
And we refused to look
We refused to take responsibility
We refused to change

God mend our wings
Heal our spirits
Forgive our beings

Amen Amen Amen

# Voices Raised In Prayer

Out of the darkness
A voice cries out
Weak and muffled
It can not shout

Lord with all Your Mercy
Lord with all Your Might
Save this unholy sinner
From the darkest night

Burdened with our demons
Crippled by our fears
Tormented by our anguish
Drowning in our tears

Lord with all Your Mercy
Lord with all Your Might
Save this unholy sinner
From the darkest night

Choices most unholy
Deeds hidden in the night
Deals with those unworthy
Promised wealth and might

Lord with all Your Mercy
Lord with all Your Might
Save this unholy sinner
From the darkest night

Lord save us from our darkness
Cleanse us from our greed
Protect us from our demons
Stop our murderous needs

Lord with all Your Mercy
Lord with all Your Might
Save this unholy sinner
From the darkest night

Lord You are the Power
Lord You are the Way
Lord Your Holy Kingdom
Brings the Light of day

Bless us with Your Holiness
Wash away our fears
Consume us with the seeds of faith
Carry us through all our years

Amen Amen Amen

# God Can You Use Me

God can You use me
I see horror all around
I hear of terror in all lands

I see Your creation dying
The people
The animals
Nature
Our world

God
I feel so helpless
I feel so sad
I feel so overwhelmed

God can You use me
I want to help
But I do not know how

God I want to give aide
But I stand motionless

God I want to carry
But I need Your help

God please use me
As an instrument
As a tool
As a light

God please give me
The strength
The courage
The faith

Please God let me help

Amen Amen Amen

# Coming Home

# Coming Home

Coming Home to Jesus
At the end of these dark days
He came here and He taught us
He showed us the Holy Ways

Returning Home to Jesus
No more these ways to roam
To the Glory of the Angels
To my Heavenly Home

Walking Home with Jesus
I choose to follow in His Ways
And worship Him as my God
Until the end of days

Amen Amen Amen

# Created By God's Hand

What a gift we have with nature
So often not realized
Taken for granted
Not seen with Holy eyes

The colors in all their splendor
The birds and insects that fly
Unique in every aspect
Do we ever wonder why

Each snow flake, it is different
Each flower's scent unique
Our lack of concern
Makes our species weak

We take so much for granted
Every life form plays a role
In this mystery of creation
In the vessel that contains the soul

How can there be such perfection
Such beauty in this land
Without the Loving Blessings
Created by God's Hand

Amen Amen Amen

# A Celebration Of Angels

Your children gather here for worship
God You are the Song our hearts sing
Our voices raised in praise most Holy
Bless us with the Fire the Holy Spirit brings

And one voice we raise to Heaven
Lord, Redeemer, Holy One
God the Song, God the Savior
Father, Spirit, Blessed Son

The Holy Spirit is in this place
God has filled us with His Grace
Our thanks we will always sing
To Jesus Christ our Heavenly King

In this place we will fill our cups with
Holiness
Our lips will taste the wine
Our hearts will be healed forever
The Fire of the Lord will be our sign

God touch all who enter here
Let this place be Your Home
Consume us with Your Presence
With You we are never alone

The Holy Spirit is in this place
God has filled us with His Grace
Our thanks we will always sing
To Jesus Christ our Heavenly King

This place is filled with Holiness
With Heaven we will commune
We surrender all to the Source
The cross will always consume

Across these plains of existence
Will our voices ring
We will join the ranks of Heaven
With the Angels, we will sing

Amen Amen Amen

# Return To Thee

When I have earned my wings of
Glory
When I have conquered all the tests
When I have learned all the lessons
When I have done my best

I will return to where I came from
The spirit and the soul
This body will be healed
No more earthly tolls

My time here was not wasted
I learned the Holy Dance
I surrendered to my God
I took the Holy chance

I let His Voice lead me
Along these dark paths
I never left His side
I conquered all the tasks

When my life in this world
Has ended for my days
I will return Home to my Father
The Son, the Spirit, Praise

Amen Amen Amen

# Amidst The Cries And Chaos

Amidst the cries and chaos
The terror and the fear
The prayers that went to Heaven
As only God can hear

And from the mist came Angels
The army that God sent
To rescue all the victims
His promises, as meant

The demons focused on the Light
And their victims did let go
As the warriors waged in battle
Their Holiness aglow

Angels in their Holiness
Stand before mankind
To save us from the darkness
To break the chains that bind

As darkness focused on the battle
The victims were set free
As a voice cried from the mist
'God fill this world with Thee'

As this battle of creation
Still wages in our lives
Do we call out to the Heavens
Or choose a world to die

Amen Amen Amen

As Darkness Focused On
The Battle
The Victims Were Set Free
As A Voice Cried From The Mist
'God Fill This World With Thee'
Amen
Amen
Amen

www.ingramcontent.com/pod-product-compliance
Lightning Source LLC
Chambersburg PA
CBHW051709040426
42446CB00008B/788